3 4028 09161 0858
HARRIS COUNTY PUBLIC LIBRARY

W9-AKD-455

Gods of Legend

ZEUS

ERIC BRAUN

BOLT

BOLT

This World Book edition of *Zeus* is published by agreement between Black Rabbit Books and World Book, Inc.

2140 Howard Dr. West,
North Mankato, MN 56003 U.S.A.
World Book, Inc.,
180 North LaSalle St., Suite 900,
Chicago, IL 60601 U.S.A.

Marysa Storm, editor; Michael Sellner, designer; Omay Ayres, photo researcher

Library of Congress Control Number: 2016049947

ISBN: 978-0-7166-9314-7

Printed in the United States at CG Book Printers, North Mankato, Minnesota, 56003. 3/17

Image Credits

Alamy: Chronicle, 10 (statue), 22 (top); Edwin Mullan, 24 (Demeter); Encyclopaedia Britannica, 22 (bottom); Encyclopaedia Britannica / Universal Images Group North America LLC, 20–21, 24 (Hestia, Hera, and Cronus), 25 (Hades, Zeus, Rhea); Entertainment Pictures, 28; Mary Evans Picture Library, 4–5; MCLA Collection, 15 (statue); World History Archive, 10 (bottom); Dreamstime: Felix Laflamme, 25 (Poseidon); Independent Artist: Mauricio Guerra, Cover, 27; Shutterstock: a Sk, 11; Danomyte, 3, 19, Back Cover; debra hughes, 24–25 (family tree); diez artwork, 28–29; Martin Capek, 15 (background); Molodec, 1; Morphart Creation, 31; Rainer Lesniewski; 12–13 (Med. map); SpinyAnt, 9 (bottom), 13 (mountain); tolietroom, 6 (rock); Vector Draco, 6 (bull); Vuk Kostic, 9 (top), 16, 32; Yuran1, 6–7
Every effort has been made to contact copyright holders for material reproduced in this book. Any omissions will be rectified in subsequent printings if notice is given to the publisher.

CONTENTS

CHAPTER 1

An Ancient Story

The god Zeus ruled over all the gods. He was powerful but easily angered. One day, he fell in love with a **nymph**. Zeus decided to kidnap her. He changed himself into a great eagle and flew her to an island.

Zeus thought nobody knew what he had done. But a human named Sisyphus saw what Zeus did. He told the nymph's father what happened. Zeus was furious.

Zeus could take many forms. In other stories, he turns himself into a swan, a bull, and a shower of gold.

Punished Forever

Zeus wanted the man to suffer for telling on him. He forced the man to push a large rock up a hill. But it wasn't just any rock. Zeus cast a spell on it. Every time the rock reached the top, it rolled back down. The man had to push it up again and again forever. Sisyphus was one of many people stories say Zeus punished.

CHAPTER 2

Greek MYTHOLOGY

The story of Zeus is a Greek **myth**. **Ancient** people told stories to explain the world. The ancient Greeks told stories about Zeus and other gods. They believed the gods made natural events happen. They believed the gods created storms. People thought the gods caused good and bad luck too.

The stories of Greek gods were written down around 750 BC. But they were told long before then.

There is a large mountain in Greece called Mount Olympus. Ancient Greeks believed the gods lived there.

Honoring Zeus

Ancient Greeks worshipped Zeus. They built **temples** and statues in his honor. The people believed worshipping Zeus would bring them good luck. Zeus controlled the sky and watched over people. If they worshipped him, people believed he would bring good weather too. He would take care of them.

Early Olympic Games were held to honor the gods.

THE ANCIENT GREEK WORLD

MOUNT OLYMPUS
highest mountain in Greece

OLYMPIA
home to the Temple of Zeus

SPARTA
powerful city-state

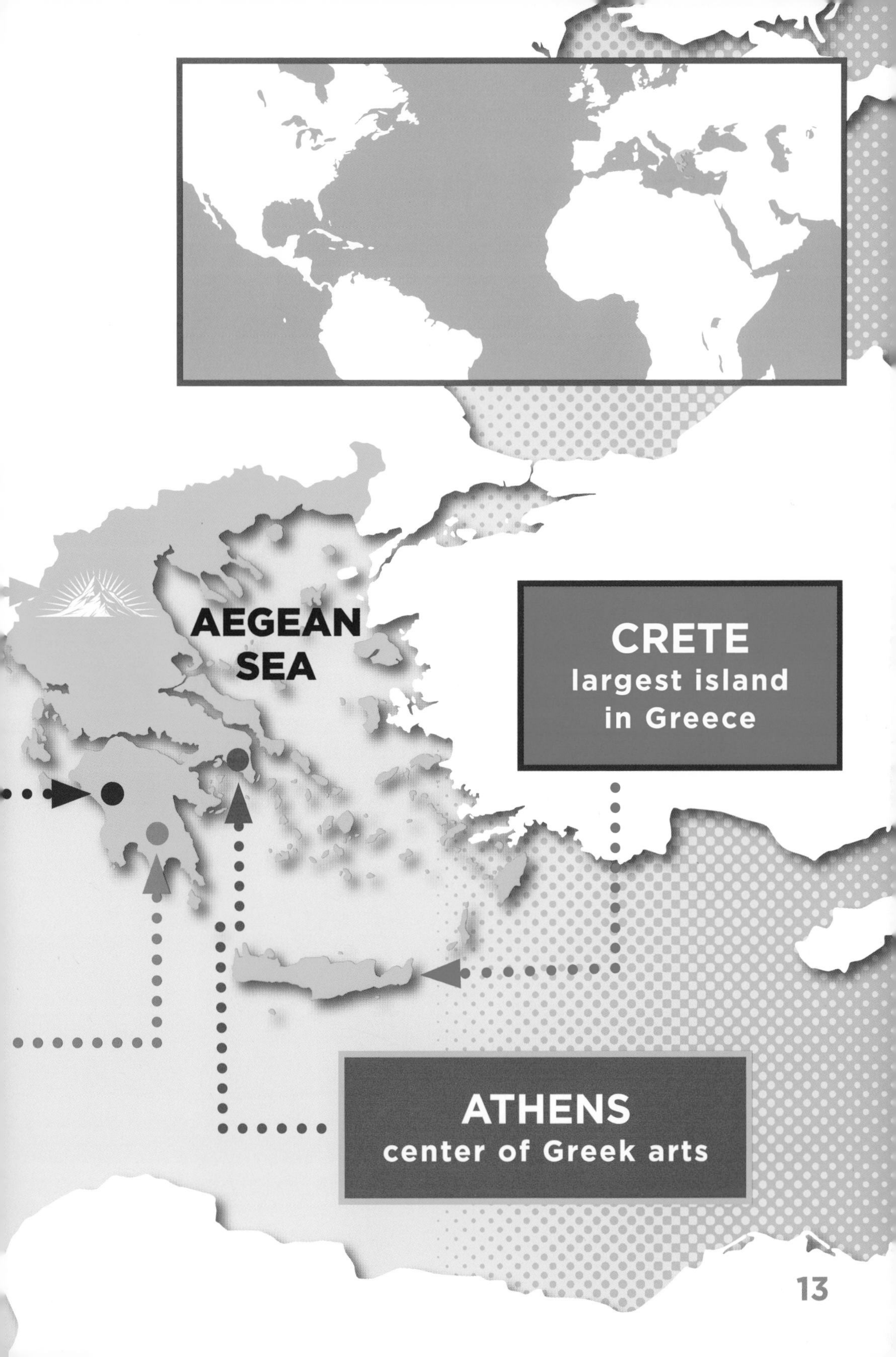
AEGEAN
SEA
CRETE
largest island
in Greece
ATHENS
center of Greek arts

CHAPTER 3

Rulers of the ANCIENT World

Myths say Zeus' father was a **Titan** named Cronus. All of the first gods came from Cronus. The Titan feared his children would take power from him. So he swallowed them when they were babies.

Battle with the Titans

Zeus' mother didn't want Zeus to be swallowed. So she hid him. When Zeus grew up, he went to Cronus. He gave his father a special drink. The drink made Cronus throw up. Zeus' brothers and sisters came out. They **defeated** their father and the other Titans.

God of the Sky and Thunder

With the Titans defeated, the gods ruled the world. Zeus became the king of all gods and humans. He was the god of the sky and thunder.

Many ancient images of Zeus show him holding a thunderbolt. He used it as a weapon in battle. He also caused lightning in the sky.

ZEUS
SCEPTER
BEARD

EASY TO ANGER
THUNDERBOLT

One story is about a Titan named Prometheus. He stole fire from Mount Olympus. He gave it to humans. This action angered Zeus. He chained Prometheus to a rock. An eagle ate his liver every day.

Anger and Justice

Stories say that Zeus watched over humans. He was wise. He settled **arguments**. And he punished those he thought deserved it. But the god's punishments could be very cruel. He punished anyone who went against him. He often punished other gods and goddesses. Many things angered Zeus.

CRONUS
a Titan
father

DEMETER
goddess of harvest
daughter

HESTIA
goddess of family
daughter

HERA
goddess of marriage
daughter

RHEA
a Titan
mother

POSEIDON
god of the sea
son

HADES
god of the underworld
son

ZEUS
god of the sky
son

CHAPTER 4

Zeus through Time

The ancient Greeks weren't the only people who told these stories. In 146 BC, the Romans defeated the Greeks. The Romans liked the Greek myths. They combined them with their own. Greek gods got Roman names. Zeus became Jupiter. The names changed, but the stories stayed mostly the same.

Same Stories, Different Names

Greek Name	Roman Name
Zeus	Jupiter
Hera	Juno
Poseidon	Neptune
Cronus	Saturn
Hades	Pluto

Zeus Today

People no longer believe the Greek gods exist. But they still enjoy the stories. Today, we see Zeus in TV shows, movies, and books. His story is very old. But it is still powerful.

ancient (AYN-shunt)—from a time long ago

argument (AHR-gyuh-muhnt)—an angry disagreement

defeat (dih-FEET)—to win a victory over

myth (MITH)—a story told to explain a practice, belief, or natural occurrence

nymph (NIMF)—a spirit in the shape of a young woman that lives in mountains, forests, meadows, and waters

temple (TEM-puhl)—a building for religious practice

Titan (TAHYT-uhn)—any one of a family of giants from ancient Greek stories

BOOKS

Cross, Gillian. *The Iliad.* Somerville, MA: Candlewick Press, 2015.

Hoena, Blake. *Everything Mythology.* Everything Series. Washington, D.C.: National Geographic, 2014.

Jennings, Ken. *Greek Mythology.* Ken Jennings' Junior Genius Guides. New York: LITTLE SIMON, 2014.

WEBSITES

5 Terrifying Tales from Greek Mythology
www.ngkids.co.uk/history/Greek-Myths

Ancient Greece: Zeus
www.ducksters.com/history/ancient_greece/zeus.php

Ancient Greek Gods
www.historyforkids.net/ancient-greek-gods.html

INDEX